Bewildered God

Bewildered God

Narayan Sahoo

Translated by
Sanjeet Kumar Das

BLACK EAGLE BOOKS
Dublin, USA | Bhubaneswar, India

Black Eagle Books
USA address:
7464 Wisdom Lane
Dublin, OH 43016

India address:
E/312, Trident Galaxy, Kalinga Nagar,
Bhubaneswar-751003, Odisha, India

E-mail: info@blackeaglebooks.org
Website: www.blackeaglebooks.org

First International Edition Published by
Black Eagle Books, 2024

BEWILDERED GOD
by **Narayan Sahoo**

Translated by **Sanjeet Kumar Das**

Original Copyright © Narayan Sahoo
Translation Copyright © Sanjeet Kumar Das

All rights reserved. No part of this publication may be reproduced, stored in a retrieval system, or transmitted, in any form or by any means, electronic, mechanical, photocopying, recording or otherwise without the prior permission of the publisher.

Cover & Interior Design: Ezy's Publication

ISBN- 978-1-64560-528-7 (Paperback)
Library of Congress Control Number: 2024933802

Printed in the United States of America

*For Swopna, My Daughter
Sujata, My Wife and
Bapa and Maa*

Critic's Opinion

The play *Bewildered God*, comprising fourteen scenes, unleashes a different taste to the readers and audience of Odia literature. In this play, the playwright Dr Narayan Sahoo has been unique and different from his earlier predecessors and contemporary playwrights of Odisha in the sense that he has tactfully and sarcastically dealt with the voice of dissent against communalism, violence and bloodshed, of human beings' religion and livelihood.

Jagannath, Ram, Ishwar, Jesus, and Allah are different names of only one omniscient, omnipotent and omnipresent soul. Though the learned pundits and experts of all religions undisputedly have accepted this view, today in Ayodhya, the Ram Mandir-Babri Masjid issue is now pan-Indic, not confined to Hindu and Muslim communities only. As the different feet of an Octopus spread in different directions, the deadly poison of communalism has infected the people and their lifestyle of entire India. Today, God is not the faith of devotees but rather a toy in man's hands, or if we speak, as stated by the playwright, Man is a master, and God is the magician to run the show as directed by the master.

The horrible Gas Tragedy had happened in Bhopal in 1984, and by that, many people were disabled, and so was Mary. She lost her procreative power. Her unfortunate husband Joseph knew this, but he couldn't express this bitter truth to Mary. The playwright has very beautifully penned down the sheer reality of life.

One day, human beings were considered as the children of God because of the presence and development of heavenly feelings in them. The cadre of attendants attached to the temple, such as priests, servitors, and administrators, were worshipped and respected in the society. But today, the Head Priest and Head Servitor in the play, engrossed in their carnal desire and longing for money, have used God as an instrument. Today, Ishwar Nivas (Dwelling Place of God) turns into a playground of pretension, deception, hypocrisy, and corruption, instead of being the storehouse of devotion and conviction,. The Head Servitor has not withdrawn himself from enjoying the bodily pleasure of *devadasi* (a female dancer attached to a temple) Leelamayee at the dead hour of night. However, the Christian Mary's youth and money are the objects of his temptation. For that reason, Mary couldn't protect herself. It was not for Mary only, but for God who was worshipped on *Ratnabedi* (the raised platform), and that His flute and *uttariya* (Shawl) the servitor has stolen is a trivial matter. At the same time, for his self-interest, this man has blamed God.

Therefore, God becomes helpless for his release from social criticisms and blemishes. It is marked that his existence is practically possible only because of the Head Priest and Head Servitor. The title of the play is properly justified. Despite this, everyone is to be tested with the touchstone of Time. Time is also an imaginary character in the play. Forfeiting God's interest, the people erect here the boundaries of communalism among them and created the mountain of religion, and are continuously engaged in inhuman activities. These are closely marked by Time and will be watched in future. Time is only the silent observer of all these happenings in the world. There will be no community, religion, deception, and hypocrisy in future- but only the supremacy of Time- with this possibility, the playwright has ended the play. As 'God' and 'Time' are characters in the play and have expressed their views, the play generates a new excitement in the hearts of the readers and viewers.

Dr. Pradeep Kumar Barik
Samanta Chandrashekhar College, Puri
Sambad 15-12.1990.

Stagecraft of Play

The theatrical performance of the play can be displayed at any stage, even at the open/thrust stage. Any 'set' for the play at the proscenium stage is unnecessary. Any director may use the 'set' on the background if needed. Dividing the scene into different zones, 'acting' can be continued.

    Zone I   : Any place

    Zone II   : Inner part of *Ishwar Nivas*

    Zone III   : Bed room of Venkatpati Raju

    Zone IV   : Leelamayee's Hall

In Zone I, the scenes that will be staged are I, II, III, IX, XII, XIII and the Last Scene.

In Zone II, the scenes that will be staged are IV, VI, X, and XI.

In Zone III, the scenes that will be staged are VII.

In Zone IV, the scenes that will be staged are V and VIII.

    The second Zone can be used for *Ishwar Nivas*, the Drawing Room and the Frontal Porch. The first Zone can be any part of the city. Sometimes, it will be deserted; at other time, it can also be crowded. It may be a road or a courtyard for the elections or any place.

Prof. Narayan Sahoo

Characterization of Play

*B**ewildered God* is an experimental play. It was broadcast and highly praised by Cuttack Akashvani Kendra in 1991. This play earned many public criticisms and was widely appreciated in public discourse.

From the very outset, I tell you that the play does not raise its voice against any religion's public sentiments. Based upon the universal feelings of the public, it's written. Here, God is not of the Hindus, Muslims, Christians, or Sikhs, but the coordinator of all religions. We may call him Krishna, Jagannath, Jesus, Allah, or Granth Sahib. On the whole, God is here an imaginary character.

Ishwar Nivas does not refer to a *devayatana* of any particular religion. God is that omnipotent Over-soul or 'the dwelling place of God'. That's why it could be better decorated. So, there is no need of set and furniture. In case of emergency, human feelings, the importance of the place, and the solemnity of the situation can be revealed through signs and symbols. 'Time' is also an imaginary character. His dress code will be bizarre and symbolic. It should be of one colour.

While considering the scenes of the courtyard of the election battle, the statues of God of different religions will be displayed through a slide show. The sound and music coming out of the background can be of any religion. The songs of any religion can be played. If one observes the announcement or news of the contemporary situation, following the different zones of the stage/play, the inner voice of the play can be convinced well.

This play was staged in Allahabad, Bhubaneswar, Burla and many other places. These were presented as the stories of *Parajita Ishwar, Asahaya Ishwar, Ashrahina Ishwar, Harijaithiba Ishwar,* etc.

Prof. Narayan Sahoo

Translator's View

People generally invoke God when they are in danger. But the play delineates the helplessness of God, who approaches human beings for help. The kaleidoscopic view of the play *Bewildered God* is adequately justified and in tandem with the present panorama of the world.

Ashra Khoji Buluthiba Ishwara, the best acknowledged and critiqued play of Narayan Sahoo and published first in 1991, is translated here as *Bewildered God*. The playwright has stated how God gets perplexed and confused to see the present situation of the contemporary world. He visits Venkatpati Raju, the *Rajashree* of *Ishwar Nivas*, and reveals his state of helplessness even in the dead of night to assist to a Christian devotee Mary who has reached this holy land from Madhya Pradesh and is raped by the Head Servitor of *Ishwar Nivas* and subsequently her dead body is found on the sea beach, but returns empty-handed. God also intimates the Administrator of the *Ishwar Nivas* for the same, and returns disturbed. Maddened at the beauty of *devadasi* Leelamayee, the Head Servitor seduces and coaxes her at midnight, when the entire city rests peacefully. Though recognized as a celestial dancer and attached to the divine soul, the *devadasi* Leela has lost her virginity because of this inhuman demoniacal servitor. In the sheath of religion, like him, others are engrossed in dirty politics and excessive carnal desire to hoodwink the world in their everyday lifestyles. Like Mary and Leela, many innocent people suffer greatly in this sordid and squalid society. They stay far behind justice.

Here, the play reinforces the politics of religions commonly manoeuvred. The people in power deceive ordinary people blatantly in the name of God or religion. They practise it habitually for their self-interest. Everywhere in the world are observed violence, anarchy, bloodshed, murder, corruption, deception and agitation. The poor and innocent voiceless succumb to the pressure the powerful cadres exert. They encounter the hegemonic groups in power and lose confidence to raise their voice appropriately.

God becomes the silent observer to watch the sly civility of the dominant group in society. The description of God referred in the play is symbolic and is not confined to any particular religion. He is the co-ordinator of all religions. To him, all religions are equal. God's compassion flows ceaselessly, irrespective of any caste, creed or colour. God, the Almighty, controls the world and never restricts Himself to any person, place and time. God and Time are two imaginary characters in the play. God is described as wounded and severely harassed in the petty politics of the modern man. Time comes to interact with God and makes Him realize that your need in society is over and your statue or idol is enough for the people to earn for their stomach.

God refers to the divine soul of any religion and may be Jagannath, Rama, Ishwar, Allah, Jesus, and Buddha. God is neither of the Hindus, the Muslims, the Christians, nor of the Sikhs only. He is above all the religions. *Ishwar Nivas* refers to any dwelling place of God. It may be the temple, mosque, church, etc. God is beautifully portrayed as the toy in the hands of the modern man who acts as the Master in the play. He behaves to the whims and calls of the Master, and at the end of the play, God is missing. Master is unaware of God's whereabouts.

God bewilders to watch the swindlers loiter helter-skelter, pronouncing their false propaganda. These cheats are not with any altruistic vision. By nature, they are self-centric. The event of the elections in the play states that they want to protect their chair (power). They are not true to the sentiments of ordinary people who lose their battle of life every moment. The torture of the ordinary person never ends. The play refers to the suffering of the workers in the aftermath of the Bhopal Gas Tragedy.

Along with the Ram-Janmabhumi Babri-Masjid issue, some other cases are considered. All these references are symbolic. Contemporary issues can be linked up with this play. So, the play's theme is of sublime order and can't be circumscribed to any particular time, place or person. It emits an evergreen light or scent.

I have tried my best to keep the language as lucid as possible. While following the rules of equivalence and the rules of fidelity between the Odia language and the English language, I came across some natural shifts. The culture-specific terms of the source language texts are maintained as they are. Some deictic expressions of the Odia language are marked in the target language while translating.

I deeply revere Professor Narayan Sahoo for believing me to translate his text carefully. He is a renowned professor of Odia Literature, retired from Utkal University. I convey my gratitude to Dr. Pradosh Kumar Swain, Assistant Professor, Department of Odia Language and Literature,

Central University of Odisha, for helping me select this text for the stuff of my work.

I convey my heartfelt gratitude to Sri Satya Pattanaik, the director of Black Eagle Books, USA and Sri Ashok Parida of the publishing house for their kind consent to publish the texts in time.

Sanjeet Kumar Das

CONTENTS

Scene I

Scene-II

Scene-III

Scene-IV

Scene-V

Scene-VI

Scene-VII

Scene-VIII

Scene-IX

Scene-X

Scene-XI

Scene-XII

Scene-XIII

Scene-XIV

Last Scene

Dramatis Personae

God	:	An imaginary Character
Master	:	Master of Magic
Time	:	An imaginary Character
Joseph	:	A devout Christian
Suleiman	:	A devout Muslim
Venkatpati Raju	:	Supreme devotee of God
Administrator	:	Manager or Trustee of *Ishwar Nivas*
Head Priest	:	Principal priest of *Ishwar Nivas*
Head Servitor	:	Principal servitor of *Ishwar Nivas*
Mary	:	Wife of Joseph
Leelamayee	:	*Devadasi* of *Ishwar Nivas*

Culture-specific Terms: *Ishwar Nivas, Devadasi, Rajashree,*

SCENE-I

[After the stage light, Master, like a magician, is seen worshiping on the stage. He is with a drum, a skull, the bone of an unmarried dead girl, and some usual things. On both sides of him are all the play's characters, standing as the audience. He gets up after worshipping. He prostrates his whole body on the ground before an image of the Goddess Bhabani. Then the words coming out of his mouth are- "*Maa*...Bhabani, *Maa*...Bhabani, I shelter at your feet." The Master stands up and beats the drum. In the meanwhile, all the characters have left the stage. Only God stays there. He shows different acrobatics in consonance with the rhythms of the drumbeats and offers his play.]

Master : (Coming to the front of the stage) Ladies, and Gentlemen! I, Biru Master, say *pranam* to you all. *Hey, Ishara* (for God), you say *pranam* to all the officers here.

God : All right.

Master : *Hey,* say pranam to them well.

God : But, I am least interested to respect them.

Master : If you do so from the very outset, they will leave the place. What will we eat? How will we live?

God	: They have all deceived me. Nobody tries to understand me. Wandering from place to place, I have displayed my shows. Have they offered me anything?
Master	: Hey, be calm and happy. They are good people. They will listen to you. They will...
God	: Well, Master! When you say, with my due respect to you, I will start soon.
Master	: (Beating the drum and after sometimes) O, Ishara, will you show the officers the magic, or will you deliver your lecture?
God	: We will show them, Master!
Master	: Which play?
God	: Magic play.
Master	: Which magic?
God	: Secret magic.
Master	: What secret?
God	: *Aainshi mantar kaainshi mantar.*
Master	: *Aainshi mantar...kaainshi mantar* 'hi'... *Aainshi mantar kaainshi mantar* 'hu'... *Aainshi mantar kaainshi mantar* 'he'...

[Master holds the skull in his hands. Sometimes, looking at the skull, unintelligible words (*mantra*) are read or uttered. After that, he revolves around the head of God three times.]

        Hey, Ishara...

God	: Yes, Master

Master	: Will we start the show?
God	: Yes.
Master	: What kind of show?
God	: What we see in our day-to-day life
Master	: Hey, what's that show?
God	: The show in which all the officers are the players.
Master	: Ladies and Gentlemen! You may think that we are here cheating you. You are wrong. We run the shows, indeed, for our belly (livelihood). I assure you all now.
	[Master fastens God's eyes with a towel so that he won't be able to see anything. God stumbles here and there, falling on the stage and getting up again.]
God	: Master, the eyes now ache. Open them.
Master	: Until you solve the officers' problems, I will keep fastening your eyes with the towel.
God	: But, Master-
Master	: *O, Ishara?*
God	: Yes, Master.
Master	: What's with this officer?
God	: A pair of spectacles in his eyes
Master	: What's that with that officer?
God	: A pen in his pocket
Master	: Why is that boy glancing backward?

God	:	Good-looking girl is sitting at his left side.
Master	:	Well, you can tell what's this in my hand?
God	:	One rupee note.
Master	:	Say, who's sitting at this side?
God	:	Mr. Gandhi
Master	:	Who's on that side?
God	:	Mr. Singh
Master	:	Who's in the front?
God	:	Mr. Lal and Mr. Nehru
Master	:	Well, say, why have they come here? Why have they come? Why? Why?

[God revolves around him very speedily. Then his feet are exhausted. When he stands unsteadily, the lights on the stage get diminished. In the dim light is heard from the mosque situated at a distance to the "Allah ho...Akbar..." sound along with the "Jay Sitaram...Jay Sitaram" sound from the temple.]

SCENE-II

[In the dim light God is observed weeping. He is wounded in the bloodshed of communalism between the Hindus and the Muslims. Trying hard frequently to get up, he fails. Crying out of distress for help, Time reaches there.]

Time	: (smiling halfway) Are you in pain?
God	: (Raising his head) Who?
Time	: Don't you recognize me?
God	: O, Time! But why are you here?
Time	: Again, the same old question? If I don't come, is there anybody in the heaven, earth, and hell to attend you?
God	: Oh...! (Being wounded)
Time	: Are you in excruciating pain?
God	: Time! Isn't there anybody to criticize?
Time	: They were all criticized here because of you. Only for you, the bloodshed happened a few hours earlier at the holy land of Ayodhya. Who is responsible for that? Answer me, God! Are you not responsible for that? Why are you silent?

God : But did I want the conflict and collision?

Time : Then, for what is this battle (*Kurukshetra*)? If you are the God of coordinating all the religions, break down that Ram Mandir (Temple of Ram)...destroy the Babri Masjid (Mosque of Babur). Let your identity alone be manifested irrespective of symbol, colour, or race. You are the Almighty! Where is your power? Why is this conflict happening here?

God : I didn't want that. But, their communal riot weakened me completely. I am tired, and disheartened!! I can't, anymore... Time.

Time : I knew, in your need, no one would attend you. Only one will come. That's only Time. Now get up..... you try to get up, shouldering upon me. Well, slowly... slowly...

[God stands holding the hands of Time.]

God : At last in the name of Religion, they have auctioned me. The words of the Gita, the Bible, the Koran, and the Granthsahib are useless and in vain.

Time : The rewards of defeat seem to be very heavy. Don't you feel, God? Anyway, those are your dues. (With a smile) Yes, yours only!

God : Time, it's not the time of joking.

Time : It's not the time of realization. The whole

	world revolts against you. They argue that your presence in this world is no longer needed. The society or world can be regulated without God (you). You are now a mere object.
God	: No, Time, no. If they lost their faith in me, this earth would be ruined. The society would move on the path of degeneration and reach hell.
Time	: The society may go to hell. The earth may be destroyed! Still, they can only be dependent upon you for a few days. Human beings are well aware of your real nature.
God	: But why?
Time	: You at least ask this question to yourself. Having faith in you, what has the man received? Only cheating…slyness…
God	: Have faith in me, Time! I have blessed them all throughout my life-span. I have always paid attention to my duties. After all this, if-
Time	: No. You have deceived them! You have made the human race eunuch, giving them the liquor of Religion! You have made them weak, helping them listen to delusive discourses of devotional Religion! You have taken away from them the food of their strength.
God	: No, Time, No! Have I done anything

wrong to save them from this materialistic world? What injustice have I done, filling their hearts with the words of truth, peace and non-violence? Tell...Time...Where's my fault?

Time : All these are cheating, full of love and devotion.

[Both of them stand like statues. At this time, from the background, is heard an announcement. After the information, they regain their earlier state.]

Announcement: "There was a conflict between the Dalits and the higher caste people in Pandatarai village, of Bilaspur district, Madhyapradesh, when the Dalits tried to enter the temple forcibly. In this riot, because of police firing, four people were neutralized, and ten of them were wounded. The state's Chief Minister has directed to make a judicial inquiry of the event."

[The event is to be read in the style of News Reading. It will be known to others that someone is reading the news.]

Time : You are equal to all, irrespective of caste, creed and colour. For what is this kind of disparity and discrimination? Why is there hatred and enmity between religions? For what is this bitterness? Please respond to my question. Is there no end to all this?

God : But, I didn't want all this?

Time : You are opportunist...selfish...You believe me. I don't know anything.

Time	: You have sponsored and facilitated this narrow casteism for ages. For you, that day, *Kalapahada* started devastating the statues in Sri Mandir. For you, in Ayodhya, mischievous activities are increased by the Hindus and the Muslims. Again for you there was bloodshed in a Gurdwara, Delhi. Now you say, for how many events will you be silent and static? Up to what Time will you behave like the lifeless objects?
God	: Please, try to understand me, Time. I don't have any role in all this. To me, there's only One Religion. That is Human Religion. Hindu, Muslim, Christian, Sikh, Jain, and Buddha are the different manifestations of the one and only one form.
Time	: Then, why, was the head of a cow thrown in the Jagannath Temple, Punjab? If temple and gurdwar were the places for prayers, why would there be a great collision and huge clamour between the Hindus and the Sikhs? Where did you hide yourself that day? For what is Kashmir bloodstained today?
God	: This selfish man always searches for me in the temples and mosques. But, my dwelling place is neither the temple nor the mosque. These are generally meant for mass prayer and meditation. The person confined to selfishness sees temple,

mosque, church and gurdwar differently. Because, in his eyes lies the collyrium of greed.

Time : You are the creation...you are the existence...you are also the best expression of progress. You watch everything; you know everything; why are you still quiet and immobile? Or are you only a propagator? Do you want to be a propagator forever?

God : No, Time; for ages, this man has misunderstood me. They have not construed my thoughts properly. I have been a means of their propaganda and publicity. But I don't expect all this from them. I want...

Time : God! There is a wide gap between what you want and what you receive. You are responsible for that. Are you not accountable for the number of violations and adulteries increasing day by day in the name of Religion? Why is Ayodhya burning today? Why is Punjab blood-faced today? Why is evergreen Kashmir bloodstained? Aren't you linked to all these issues?

God : I don't have any link to the issues cited above, Time. I am One. I have one form. But for them, I have many forms. Tell me, have I passed them this idea? In the beginning of Creation I was. Today, I am too. I am the central point of that heavenly

	experience. But today's man has forgotten me. My senseless form (Idol) matters to them. My name is enough for them. I have been a word for them.
Time	: Your confidence level has been weakened, God. From now onwards, you can't be relied upon.
God	: But, I have never poisoned or diluted their faith. I have always supported and respected them. Where is my fault?
Time	: Then, for what was Biswabashu's belief diluted? He was the representative of the Dalit community? Wasn't it? Could he not arrange a bed of pride and abundant food for you? Could he not organize thirteen festivals in twelve months? What had you given him for this in return?
God	: Understand me, Time. I don't have any fault in this.
Time	: You can't be trusted. You are the supporter of Capitalism! You have never been of the poor and the oppressed. You have always supported those who have given you the comfortable beds for ages.
God	: Believe me, Time! I am the friend and relative of the poor and the fallen. I have been with them for the establishment of truth and peace in the society. I am their friend.
Time	: You are an apostle of peace! Then tell me,

	for what was Martin Luther martyred that day? For what did Socrates take poison? For what was Mohan Das Karamchand Gandhi fired at the Prayer Hall? Respond to me.
God	: How can I help you understand, Time? What has happened or is happening in this world is executed in my name only. I don't have any direct link with that. They are using my name frequently.
Time	: From an individual, your need ends, God! You will be converted into a useless object immediately.
God	: Don't say like that, Time. I am not the culprit. They have used my name for their interest and their benefit. They are also using.
Time	: I feel very sorry for you, God! Man becomes self-conscious. The day he will be fully conscious, your name will be erased from the earth. You can't tame and pacify him with your magical spell. You can't trap him with the antidote of faith.
God	: No…Time…No…Don't distort the beliefs of an individual. He will live, with beliefs…with devotion…with truth…with peace…

[God breaks down entirely in sadness. A streak of smile is perceived in Time's face. The stage lights gradually dim.]

SCENE-III

[There is no light on stage. When the Master is found playing the instrument, the light dispels darkness gradually. Master comes to the front of the stage. Playing of instrument is stopped. Master reads out his traditional sermon.]

Master : Ladies and Gentlemen! You must have been annoyed with me in the meantime. I have misled you so long. No, as we earn money from you, we will show you the magic. No need to be worried, I will show you some playful events. Then, the play is yet to be started. What you have seen is just a trailer.

The quarrel about God and the temple is observed in almost all the countries of the world. Sometimes it is between the Gita and the Bible; sometimes, it is between the Hindu and the Muslim. The conflict happens between religions and between castes. This play starts with an event of this kind. You can think of the play's origin, at any dwelling place of God. It may be either a temple or mosque or a church or gurdwar. God is merely a symbol. He may be of any religion. Then, let's see what has happened and what will happen…

[While Master starts playing the instrument, the light gets slightly dimmed. Master has left the stage. Slight darkness pervades the stage. Then the sound of a bell is heard in the church, and in the air is echoed the voice of a Father at a distance.]

Father : (From the background) "O God! You pardon these vile children. What we do is for our self-interest. Because of our selfishness, we do something wrong intentionally. So, you forgive us for not following the path you have directed. Please show us the light."

[By the time light comes, Joseph is walking on the stage disturbed. He is a Christian middle-aged man. He seems to be engrossed in thoughts.]

Joseph : Father, I can help others understand. But, how can I say it to Mary-"She can no longer be a mother." Union Carbide Gas has taken away her motherhood completely. I can't…I can't…

[Joseph talks to himself.]

Mary : (Entering) Can't you do?

[Mary is Joseph's wife and a follower.]

Joseph : Nothing.

	[Joseph does not expect Mary's presence there.]
Mary	: Have you returned so early? What's about compensation? Will it be provided to all?
Joseph	: If Lord Jesus comes down to help the earth, the sufferings of people in Bhopal Gas tragedy can't end.
Mary	: You don't say so. Let Lord Jesus remove the sufferings from all.

[Both of them stand like statues. Then, one stanza of the saint's poem, Bhima Bhoi, is heard from the background. After the song, that stage of silence will disappear. A song of any religion can be incorporated.]

> "The sorrows and agonies of all beings are infinite,
>
> Who can tolerate seeing them?
>
> Let my life (soul) be in the hell,
>
> Let the world be saved."

Joseph	: The compensation scheme the Government has declared to provide is actually a drop in the ocean.
Mary	: How long will we wait and stay here for the government relief? At least do something for us. Otherwise-
Joseph	: I can't think of what to do next. I am completely helpless and hopeless, keeping in view the loss.

Mary	: Today, Rahmat Miyan left this colony forever and went home with his daughter. While leaving, Pratima cried very much. You saw in your eyes how Gurubachan Singh, with his children, left for Punjab, his native land.
Joseph	: All will leave one by one. Those who left the world had been saved from danger. But the cursed people are alive; more than two lakh people are disabled physically. But, as per the Government Report, the number is only forty thousand. Some have lost their eyes, while some are without the uterus. Somebody's kidney stops functioning, while another's liver is non-functional. How many days will they fight with death? Oh...Lord, forgive us! Forgive us!
Mary	: Joseph, let's return to our village. Half of the colony has already left. We lead our terrible life here.
Joseph	: Yes, Mary, we will do that. Union Carbide has disabled one of my eyes. Still, I am with the other eye. We won't face any want in our life.
Mary	: Joseph, what has the doctor said about your eye?
Joseph	: What else will he say? I am told what others have already been told. Repenting of that won't bring any good result.
Mary	: Yes, Nazma went to the hospital with her

husband. The doctor said, "She can't be a mother." Her two grown-up children died. She, the most unfortunate, was with patience for the next issue. But that doctor's report, ...

[Joseph is shocked.]

Joseph : Mary, who says you to live with all these negative thoughts in your mind? If you are good, the whole world will be good.

Mary : Lord Jesus! Let the helpless people have patience to live...give them courage. (Doing a prayer to Jesus)

Joseph : Nazma is not the only one. Thousands of Nazmas suffer from the same problem. Who will relieve them?

Mary : I don't want to stay here for a moment, Joseph. I feel terribly bad.

Joseph : Yes...we will certainly return. But I think about my aunt. She loved Laura very much. When she will search for Laura, how will I reply? Can I tell her that Bhopal Gas Tragedy has taken her granddaughter away forever? No, Mary, I can't. How can I say this story?

Mary : Don't be sad at all. We will forget everything gradually. As the parents we have tolerated this great loss, so why can't she?

Joseph : She is an octogenarian woman. How can I help her understand this, Mary? Sometimes later-

Mary	: No! (Mary starts crying.) You don't say so. Or else, I will do suicide.
Joseph	: Mary!
	[He reveals the fact inadvertently and carelessly.]
Mary	: Tell me the fact, for my sake. Is it mentioned in the doctor's report? Tell me whether I can be a mother or not.
	[Mary breaks down in sadness. She seems to be tired.]
Joseph	: Mary, who said, you can't be a mother?
Mary	: You said.
Joseph	: Did I say? No…Yes, Mary. Anyway, let me know what we will take for my aunt.
	[He tries to curb the conversation.]
Mary	: Don't mislead me. What's the medical report? I still doubt. Tell me.
Joseph	: Hey, there's nothing wrong, a slight weakness.
	[Joseph tries to console her.]
Mary	: Do you try to hide it from Mary? Say, for my sake. (Joseph remains silent.) Why don't you say? Tell…for Lord Jesus' sake.
Joseph	: No, …Mary…No,…I am helpless…I am helpless.

[Joseph clasps Mary. Their eyes are full of tears. The lights get dimmed on stage.]

SCENE-IV

[It's now a sacred place of any religion. It's the dwelling place of God. The inside view of that abode is considered. God is installed permanently on the raised platform. On both sides of God are sitting Venkatpati Raju, Administrator, Head Priest and Head Servitor. In front of God, a *devadasi* (dancing girl attached to the temple) Leelamayee dances for God.]

Head Priest : Wah, mind-blowing! Gorgeous dance!

Head Servitor : Superb! Leelamayee's graceful style is very marvellous!

[Venkatpati Raju smiles mentally. He also follows her.]

Administrator : *Rajashree* (Royal Sage), today's dance has been full of excitements.

Venkatpati Raju : All that's of God's greatness.

[Any classical song of Jayadev or any other poet that suits the dance can be incorporated.]

Head Servitor : Rajashree, Leelamayee's dance today, has surpassed and broken all her previous records.

Head Priest : That's not all. A divine smile seems to glisten in God's face! It's very rare and extra-ordinary.

[While dancing, she falls down at God's feet. Still, God is immovable and silent.]

Venkatpati Raju : Blessed...blessed, Leelamayee! You are blessed!

Administrator : O God's female companion, you are a celestial nymph (dancer) on this earth.

[Having seen Leelamayee falling, the Head Servitor gets hold of her. He sprinkled padodaka (water with which an idol has bathed.) over her body. Leelamayee regains her consciousness.]

Venkatpati Raju : Leelamayee! Today, your dance has pleased all of us. There is a strange magical power in your dance.

Leelamayee : All that's of most compassionate God's blessing. I accomplish my duties only.

(The bells and gongs ring at this time. Raju and all the councillors stand up. God disappears in the meantime. Saying Namaskar to Raju, Leelamayee leaves.)

Head Priest : Yes, devotee best! The Government has sanctioned one lakh rupees only for preparing *prasad* (offerings made to a deity). You are aware of the amount we spend every year in the service to God.

Head Servitor : The salary for male and female servitors is only eight lakhs. If it continues, there will be certainly indiscipline.

Venkatpati Raju	:	Then you tell me what I can do?
Administrator	:	You please write a letter to the Collector regarding this. Express your statements in the newspapers.
Head Priest	:	His Majesty! You are an incarnation of God. You are saint...you are King, if you want, everything will be set right.
Venkatpati Raju	:	Yes, Incarnation! Royal Saint! A sheer amount of dust is stored on the throne. I have never tried to clean it. I have adjusted myself. It's as usual. Why will I clean? What's the benefit?
Head Servitor	:	*Rajashree* (Royal Saint)! Though there is no monarchy, you are still our crownless King. You are also God's best devotee. God depends on you.
Venkatpati Raju	:	Yes (taking a long breath)! Nobody is obstructed to tell a person in the outer cover of the monarchy a 'King', because the King is an ordinary man. He is an obedient citizen of democracy.
Administrator	:	Rajashree! Now, on this earth, millions of people respect you. They bow their heads down before you and will do in future too.
Venkatpati Raju	:	After the monarchy is over, nobody is '*Praja*' (subject) here. All are treated equal as '*janata*' (ordinary people). They are the citizens of an independent province. Out of them, only one person is honoured as '*Rajashree*'.

Head Priest : His Majesty! To our eyes, you are not a man but God. You are our Master. Nowadays, the Government has taken the responsibility of maintenance of this sacred place, but for ages, with your donations, this holy place has been cared for.

Venkatpati Raju : Camphor has gone; what's left is only the cloth. After some days, that will also vanish.

Administrator : The degree of indiscipline is increased since the day the Government has taken the responsibility of the *'Ishwar Nivas'* (dwelling place of God). Every day, one can see the conflicts in this holy land.

Head Priest : Following the Govt. rules, the administration of *'Ishwar Nivas'* will be run, not the daily rituals offered to God. For this, we need the purification of the heart and holy surroundings.

Head Servitor : Nobody in our family has received any salary for the last fourteen generations. They all depended on *jagiri* (grant of rent-free land for service rendered). But, today, we are deprived of that because of the Government. We are today salaried servants.

Head Priest : How much are we paid to do the ritual services to God? We are Govt. servants.

Venkatpati Raju : Yes (Taking a long breath). Royal Palace is now used as the Govt. Administrative

Office and Rajashree (the Royal Saint) is turned into a servant to depend upon Government Salary.

All of them : 'Rajashree'...

[Raju breaks down in sorrow and anger. His head bows down. The stage is lit off.]

SCENE-V

[This is the residence of dancer Leelamayee. It's midnight. The courtyard smells with sweet fragrance. Head Servitor has come with a rose-flower bouquet.]

Head Servitor : Leelamayee...Leela...My sweetheart...

Leelamayee : (Coming out) *Sevak Maharaj,* your visit at midnight...

Head Servitor : Why will I show my hypocrisy? (Giving her the bouquet)

Leela : I say this for your honour and prestige. You are the Head Servitor to God.

If you come to *Devadasi* Leelamayee's residence at midnight,...

Head Servitor : The tranquility pervades everywhere in the city. All are taking rest. God must have slept. The festivities have been over very early.

Leela : Does this message spread from ear to ear? As I am born in hell, so, to me, the smell of drains is the scent of sandalwood. But, how come you are here? You are the most respected fellow of the temple!

Head Servitor : Leela, I can't live for a moment without you.

	Let others say what they want, but I am- [He proceeds to embrace her.]
Leela	: A little excitement can bring someone to the path of degeneration. Control yourself, at least. We have enough time.
Head Servitor	: Then, our frequent interactions…our love and friendship? Do you reject all this?
Leela	: Whose body has already been surrendered to God, to love for her is a valueless object. Love for her is a great thought. It's not so easy to touch that.
Head Servitor	: No…Leela…No…Does your heart say this, Leelamayee? I know my Leela very well.
Leela	: Servitor, the best! You have time. If you want, you can correct yourself. You can control your inner flow. Again, to be emotional is not good for you.
Hear Servitor	: Who will obstruct the path of fluvial river…rolling stone…burning fire? My heart, mind and soul…everywhere are your vibrations. Tell me, "How can I live barring me?" My life is impossible without you.
Leela	: 'But'…(disturbed)
Head Servitor	: Don't obstruct me. Let the streams of two fluvial rivers mingle with the infinite sea. You will see, there is another life out of this earth. You will feel and realize this. How beautiful that life is! How dreamful, how generous, how nobler that flow is!

Leela	: I am God's *devadasi* (celestial dancer devoted to God). I am completely devoted to Him in my body, mind and speech. Nobody can get a place in my mind except Him. You know it very well.
Head Servitor	: How much will you restrain yourself to the rules and the riddles of Religion? Will the scriptures provide you any solution for the demands of your body? Can God pacify your hunger?
Leela	: 'But', my mind- (She is unsteady and disturbed)
Head Servitor	: The notion of vice and virtue is an unconditional belief for man. I am a servitor as per the weighing scale of Religion. But, after all, I have an identity too. That's of a social being. I have my body, mind, heart and youth. All these are for you only.
Leela	: Now everything is within the ambit of my hall, I can't accept. The *laxman rekha* (borderline) drawn before me ridicules me sarcastically. I can't...I can't...
	[Leelamayee breaks down. She is unable to decide what to do.]
Head Servitor	: Those are the delusions of the mind. Tell me, the God for whom you burn yourself bit by bit, has He ever thought of the hidden feelings of a woman, her words, and her heart's sorrows and agonies? Could you answer me?

Leela	: Servitor best! (in a painful voice)
Head Servitor	: Bitter truth is always painful. For how many days will you dance in the name of celestial nymph/*devadasi*? Having seen other women in the society, aren't you with any reaction? Is your motherhood not excited, having seen the children of others? Aren't you a woman? Aren't you a mother?
Leela	: 'Servitor, the great'...! (Closing eyes in heavenly bliss)
Head servitor	: No, Leela, you'd rather call me Nandu.
Leela	: 'Nandu'...(in happiness) what a pleasure! What a peace! Nandu...
Head Servitor	: Yes, Leela! For so many days, you spend your life like a blind fellow. Now you have explored the right path. It depends on you how to march ahead. Time waits for none. The road is open before you.
Leela	: I will march ahead, Nandu! I will undoubtedly move on. When I have experienced the first sunlight, I won't miss it anymore. I will drink it to the fullest.
Head Servitor	: Are you speaking the truth?
Leela	: I promise you...

[Both of them have clasped each other! For sometimes, they have been mesmerized. In the meantime, while the stage light is off.]

SCENE-VI

[It's now the entrance gate of God's dwelling place. There is continuous movement of the people through the gate. A devotional song is heard from that place. "Alone your Devotee's life-" more stanzas of the lyrical hymn may be sung. In the middle of the song, the people raise their hands. The music may be of any religion.]

Head Servitor : (At the entrance gate) Hello, you are not dropping a single penny. Why are you rushing here? Hey, all these are Madhias (poor people). None of them is a gentleman!

[Joseph and Mary are marked at a distance from the entrance gate. In their hands are two oversized, heavily loaded items (bundles). They try to take a rest, keeping somewhere. Head Servitor eyes that.]

Head Servitor : They reached...the devotees moved. I have waited for you two only. Why are you late? Devotee best! Please come now.

Joseph : Namaskar, Sir?

Mary : Namaskar, Sir?

Head Servitor : Where are you from?

Joseph	: From Bhopal.
Head Servitor	: It's marked by your style of movement. Be aware of the pickpockets here. Keep your purse safe.
Joseph	: We have kept it rightly. Does it happen at the holy place?
Head Servitor	: Surely, God is here, but what about the people working here? How will they live?
Mary	: Head Servitor! Is worshipping God completed? Please help us-
Joseph	: We are from a far-off place. Please be compassionate to us.
Head Servitor	: That means…that means…that means…I understand…no need to say more. You are truly the devotees! Well, if you give money, everything is possible. How much virtue do you need?
Mary	: Servitor best! We have come here with a solemn vow in our minds. I am Mary, and he is my husband, Joseph.
Head Servitor	: (Looking downward silently)
Joseph	: Why are you silent abruptly? We have come from a long distance. Please help us. Today, we have to return. Our native place is in a different state.
Mary	: Please, don't harass us; Servitor best! We will give you your dues. You will receive the amount you want, but please make some arrangements for us.

Head Servitor	: (Still silent)
	[Looking at the surroundings hastily]
Joseph	: What happens, Servitor best? Why don't you say anything?
Head servitor	: As you are from a different Religion, both of you can't visit the dwelling place of God? Leave the place quickly. If anybody sees-

[Before they leave, Mary requests the Head Servitor with humble submission by touching his feet.]

Joseph	: Servitor best, please help us. Otherwise, our hopes will remain unfulfilled.
Head Servitor	: Leave…leave…leave my feet. Both of you are Christians. You can't see God. Only the Hindus can see God. His *nivas* (dwelling place) is prohibited for you.
Joseph	: But why? God is for everyone! He is for all religions. Your scripture says this. You have all decided this.
Mary	: Servitor best! Please help us. We have come here with many hopes. Can our visit from Bhopal will be fruitless?
Head servitor	: I can't do anything. Only the Hindus have the right to enter the temple here. If anybody sees me talking to you, it will be inauspicious. Leave the place as quick as possible. If you want your life, don't come here again.
Mary	: If you want, every impossible can be made possible.

Head servitor	: I have told you that I can't. Hey, you don't have the right to enter. How can I help you?
Mary	: Then, will my hopes be my hopes only?
Joseph	: Why do we publicize and preach that God is the coordinator of all religions? Why is this hypocrisy? For what is this kind of deception?
Head Servitor	: You are a sinner. Otherwise, why is one of your eyes lost? You are saying a lot! Quit the place immediately.
Joseph	: Why is this hypocrisy and deceitfulness in the name of Religion? Why do you campaign for the God of the world, as the regulator, and the world leader? How many days will you hoodwink the people in the name of Religion?
Head Servitor	: Hey, do you teach me what the spiritual knowledge is? We have been serving God here for the last fourteen generations. Do you want to teach me the principles? O, the disciple of Jesus! Leave the place. Quit immediately.
Joseph	: Mary, haven't I told you? God is for the Hindus only here. If we visit, we won't have any benefit. He only listens to the Hindus. He is the hired God of the Hindus.
Mary	: You don't say so. Salabega, a muslim also received compassion of Lord Jagannath.

	If Jagannath blesses Salabega, why can't we be blessed?
Joseph	: No…these are all pretensions. This is not a temple but a rendezvous for the Hindus. It is heard that God is the coordinator of all religions. But I see today- these are all misconceptions and lies, only deceptions. The devotees are baffled and befooled here in the name of Religion.
Head Servitor	: What do you see, the sinner? Don't you hear me? Will you leave the place? Or else I will call…?
Joseph	: The priests and servitors have exclusive monopoly of God; He is the hired God of the Hindus only. We have made a mistake visiting this holy place.
Head servitor	: A stupid…a sinner…an atheist! I will uproot your tongue if you speak one more word against God. Will I call the ruffians?
Joseph	: How many days will you show your supremacy, controlling Religion? Only for this had *Kalapahad* invaded Jagannath Temple? O Lord! For how many days will you be a ball (to be played) in the hands of priests and servitors? Why are you silent? Is there no end to this? Is there no end to this malice?
Mary	: Please stop for a while! For my sake, please stop.
Joseph	: No, Mary,….it's enough! We have to

revolt against this injustice. I have to prove that God is for all the people...for all religions...for all communities. He has never been of *Maulavis, Mullahs, Purohits* and Priests only.

Head Servitor : A sinner! Do you know how much we have to pay for you? The number of people coming earlier to you raised their voices here are in the asylum till date. I may be cursed for you! You can think of Jesus in one slap only.

Mary : No...Servitor best, please pardon him, at least for me.

Head Servitor : I am the Head Servitor of the Lord Jagannath here. My insult means the insult to the entire Hindu community. If I want, a drop of blood of this sinner won't be seen here. He won't return to his place alive.

Mary : No, Servitor best! You can pardon us. It's our fault.

Joseph : We can return instead; what will we get, thinking of these *Jaradagavas*?

Head Servitor : Only for you, I leave this sinner. If you want, you can see God alone, but not through the main door. You have to enter through the back door. Nobody will see you enter. Do you agree?

Mary : (Supplicating the answer from Joseph) What do you say? I enter. Stay here with our luggage. I will come back soon. Having reached here, will we return empty-handed?

Head Servitor : Come...don't be late. If anybody knows, I have to face the music.

[Both Head Servitor and Mary enter. Joseph looks at them earnestly. He knows very well that he can't help Mary understand this.]

SCENE-VII

[It's the midnight. Venkatpati Raju has slept deeply. God reaches his chamber. A slight dim light casts on the room/stage. The king dreams of. The dream-sequence is shown. After God comes in, the light sheds upon *Rajashree* (the royal saint). Raju would get up from the bed, as if he were hypnotized.]

V. Raju	: You are in the dead of night! You could have invited me! Why have you reached here walking hard, though the servitors and priests are in your dwelling place? Is there any emergency at night?
God	: I have been forced to visit you, Venkatpati Raju! But, you promise me.
V. Raju	: Please tell me what happens. You seem to be disturbed.
God	: I have been ruined, Raju! Everything is lost in my devotion.
	[He can't speak anything. He breaks down.]
V. Raju	: Tell me frankly, Lord. How can I know if you don't say? I am not the omniscient

	like you. Why do you pretend before the devotee?
God	: Head Servitor has ruined my devotee. To her he...I want the remedy, Raju.
V. Raju	: Lord, how come it happened to your devotee in your presence? You couldn't do anything?
God	: After raping (ruining the purity of) my devotee, Head Servitor has murdered her by squeezing the neck. A sinner...a mean person...
V. Raju	: Lord, if it's true, its consequence will be dreadful. After knowing all this, how did you come to me?
God	: Yes, for help! I know very well that you can help me.
V. Raju	: But...
God	: Don't question 'but', Venkatpati Raju. The dead body of my devotee Mary is still on the sea beach. If you want-
V. Raju	: Lord, how did it happen?
God	: Both husband and wife, my devotees, came here from Bhopal with many hopes. Head Servitor, taking Mary for my visit, raped her. Mary's husband still sits waiting for her return at the entrance gate. How can I console him?
V. Raju	: But, how can I help you, Lord? When you are unable to help them, how can I help them?

God	:	Please help Mary's dead body reach Joseph from the sea beach. He has been completely broken down. You can do this work. I have faith and conviction in you.
V. Raju	:	'But'-
		[Raju asks questions to himself.]
God	:	No question of 'but' is to be raised, Raju! You are my devotee, the greatest, and the best. Help my devotee at this critical moment. Do the arrangement to punish the Head Servitor. I know that he won't dishonour your words.
V. Raju	:	Lord, don't you know my condition here? I am only a dormant representative of the lost monarchy. As per the request of tradition, I am only a royal saint. But, you know my true nature.
God	:	No, Raju! You don't say so. If you want, you can do a lot. Who will I go to?
V. Raju	:	My power is also limited, Lord. The rules and regulations of the Government have shackled my hands and legs. I am confined to the boundaries of your dwelling place, administrator, and priest. I can't go an inch beyond this. They harness my movement.
God	:	But, many people in the country respect you with utmost devotion, Venkatpati Raju! Your heart is generous; your mind is broad. You can't do this for that mass.

V. Raju : Because of their request, I have been made a puppet. I am only a common man depending upon the Govt. salary! My rights are limited. Venkatpati Raju has donated everything for God's dwelling place and does not have anything now. I am helpless...I am a destitute/penurious. What can I give to you?

God : You can, Venkatpati! You wake up for your beloved God. You start generating faith in others.

V. Raju : Today, man does not have any faith in me, as Saddam Hussein has opened his eyes. Scud and Patriot are his persons to be believed in. Devotion won't help him anymore. He needs only power.

God : If you want, you can solve many problems. You are the Servitor to the common people. You are my supreme devotee.

V. Raju : All my wishes and desires are dedicated to the country. The ordinary people's hopes and aspirations are my compulsory duties. Venkatpati Raju works with a pension amount. Please tell me, Lord, what I am with to give you after all my power or freedom are withdrawn? I have been entirely helpless, Lord. Aren't you happy to see me in this poor and dejected state?

God : Raju, don't break down your heart. Though camphor is gone, the cloth is left. There is still a taste in it. Keep that taste alive. You will live for me and my devotees.

V. Raju : Yes (taking a long breath), that taste won't benefit the person named Raju residing in the hopeless surroundings of this diseased palace. Democracy has dishonoured me. I will never forgive them. I have not done any injustice to the people! I have never betrayed them!

God : Don't you respect 'Democracy'? Do you not have any faith in democracy?

V. Raju : I respect. I expected to receive reasonable dues. But what did I get? For how many days will I live, taking into account the temple and idols? How will I live? My case is still sub judice at the Honourable Supreme Court.

God : But, as per your direction, God's dwelling place is regulated. Barring you, what's its existence?

V. Raju : As per the traditional belief system, I am here only the representative of God. But, all my works are controlled. Please tell, Lord, how many days will I be a toy in the hands of the ordinary people? I will give my signature. They will execute and exercise power. For how many days will I be the rubber stamp?

God : The Creation is passing through a very critical time. Had it not been the case, the

	injustices wouldn't have happened one after another. With your request only, that day, disowning Nature, I came here for the ordinary people.
V. Raju	: I have remembered all that, Lord. I made the whole arrangement to establish you in the world durbar. From that day onwards I had been with unlimited power. I was the King. But today I am *Rajashree* (the royal saint).
God	: Had I come to you for this? Had you not promised me to flood the world-friendship on this earth irrespective of caste, creed and colour? Had you not told me to arrange places for Hindus, Muslims, Jains and Christians at my dwelling place?
V. Raju	: Time has overpowered me, Lord. Monarchy is over, but a man named Rajashree lives here only to drink the last poison of devastated democracy.
God	: Day by day at my place, the mischievous activities of the priests and the servitors are increasing. Today, cheating the people in the name of Religion has become a rule. You must think of it, Venkatpati!
V. Raju	: When the controller or Creator of the world is helpless, what can I do more? Don't you see how I am unable to touch your devotee's dead body? I know everything...I am still helpless.

God : I have to make some arrangements before the night ends. Then I leave, Raju.

[Raju says Namaskar to God. God leaves the place! In that faded light, Raju comes back to his bed. When the light becomes normal, Raju was shocked, as if he were dreaming of so long.]

SCENE-VIII

[This is the House of *devadasi* Leelamayee. It's the midnight. The royal dancer and Head Servitor of Ishwar Nivas (Dwelling place of God) are engrossed in dance and music. In the middle of the dance, the inebriated Head Servitor hobbles. He can't maintain his balance. So he stands still at a place.]

Leela : Today, you have accepted your defeat so early! Oh……

Head Servitor : I am also happy in getting defeated by the royal dancer. That defeat is also a victory to me.

[Head Servitor looks at Leelamayee's face attentively. Her face glistens.]

Leela : Ye…Ye…! O…why do you look at me so earnestly?

[Head Servitor became normal as if he were dreaming so long.]

Head Servitor : Yes, I watch you…I also think of you. How come so many styles and desires get stored in an individual?

Leela : Today, you are under the spell of excessive inebriation. Otherwise-

Head Servitor : Leela, you look so gorgeous today! More beautiful and smarter than the earlier times! How gorgeous you are tonight! How beautiful you are!

Leela : Perhaps your pocket is full now! Otherwise, no words will come out of your mouth. If the bags of servitors and priests weighed more, they would love to use this kind of literary expression. Am I wrong? Am I telling you the lies?

[Leelamayee speaks very lovingly and erotically. The inebriated Head Servitor enjoys and accepts Leela's flattery pleasantly.]

Head Servitor : Truly speaking, Leela, I don't like to leave you alone even for a minute. Till the time I am here, I feel that I am in heaven.

Leela : Who have you cheated today? How much have you received? Who's the prey? Can I know whether male or female?

Head Servitor : Honestly speaking, Laxmi! I promise thrice. I have none except you. What I do is only for you.

Leela : Hold on, you don't flatter more, Servitor, the great! Others may be unaware, but I know you very well.

Head Servitor : Believe me, Leela. Only for you, forgetting the darkness of night, I come here. The rules and regulations of *Ishwar Bhavan* are the thorns in my path today. Only the night's darkness has cleared my path. In

	that path, I can see your bright face only, Leela! Come on and embrace me, Leela!
Leela	: Everybody appreciated me greatly on the 'Dance Platform' that day. I can recollect everything one by one. I am a royal dancer. Throughout my life, I have received appreciation and accolades.
Head Servitor	: Your dance was uncommon and extraordinary that day. Everybody accepts this freely and publicly.
Leela	: But I did expect something more from you. It should have been something different and something special. But you have harassed me that day!
Head Servitor	: I have already given you everything. My mind…heart…soul… I have nothing now to give to you. Tell me what you expected. Will you be happy if you get that?
Leela	: Had I wished that, Leelamayee would have received from anybody. But, you were the principal traveler of my goal. So, I wanted that business-
Head Servitor	: Tell me why you are silent. What did you want that day? Hiding from me, will you earn anything? I am only yours.
Leela	: This poor dancer had many expectations from his near and dear ones. I had no dearth of money. I had received a lot from the *Ishwar Nivas*. I had earned my name and fame. Wealth Jewels and money- I

was not satisfied with all these. I wanted from you-

Head Servitor : Is this Head Servitor with something that can't be given to you, Leela? You tell, my sweetheart. For whom is the Head Servitor unmarried, today? For whose attraction do I come to the courtyard of dancer Leelamayee, breaking the rules and regulations of the *Ishwar Nivas*? Who do I come for?

Leelamayee : Till the time the servitors are under the spell of sexual desire, the moral lessons of this kind are heard from them. I am well-acquainted with this type of coaxing.

Head Servitor : Believe me, Leela. I am only yours. Yes, Leela, yours only.

Leela : Once the 'sexual desire' calms down, it is as the former and the ultimate. I have known you well, Head Servitor.

Hear Servitor : I have nothing to give you except helping you believe. Please tell me what you want from me.

Leela : Had you wanted, I would have been yours.

Head Servitor : Believe me, Leela. You are the first and last woman of my life. I don't have any love relationship with other woman till date.

Leela : This coaxing has been very old to me. Why will I give any more coats to it? Instead, you come down to the real world.

Head Servitor : Leelamayee, You are then to me-

Leela : I understand you well, but you have misunderstood me. I don't want wealth and prosperity. I am the only dancer attached to God. What I receive from *Ishwar Nivas* is enough for me to live.

Head Servitor : The mind's hunger is not satisfied at worshipping God, Leela. The urge gets intensified as time goes on. As we grow up with time, the 'demand of body' and the 'desire of mind' multiply.

Leela : Still, I have tried to forget all this, looking at God's face. But only for you, I have an intense storm in my mind. You have created that storm. Today, I have been absent-minded for you. I have stepped on a different path for you. But what have I received? I was rather happy in my lonely life…the life of the royal dancer…the life of the dancer attached to God.

Head Servitor : The heart's thirst is pacified with cold water but not the mind's desire. Your understanding is completely wrong. You don't know what fullness is?

Leela : The fate of all the dancers attached to God is under that stone. They are all incomplete women forever. Their incompleteness is for the destiny of their work and the cause for ages.

Head Servitor : No, Leela…No…

Leela	: In this society, the dancers devoted to God are not women but are cursed statues or idols. Otherwise, that day you-
Head Servitor	: Leelamayee, you gradually become mysterious! Your mystery tortures me a lot, Leela!
Leela	: Truth is always painful. Tell me Servitor best, Can you give me rebirth? Rebirth... Freedom...
Head Servitor	: I can't understand, Leela. Clarify me what you want.
Leela	: Can you marry me publicly in the courtyard of God tomorrow? Can you consider me as your wife?
Head Servitor	: Leela! (Getting surprised) Have you given a second thought to what you say? I am the Head Servitor of *Ishwar Bhavan*. The prestige of *Ishwar Bhavan* depends on my position and reputation. How can I work going beyond rules and principles? Will this Creation exist? A terrible injustice!
Leela	: Is there any rule that you can meet secretly and have a physical relationship with *devadasi* (dancer) of God in the darkness of night? What kind of justice is this? You are selfish...Cheat and swindler. Go away and leave me alone.
Head Servitor	: Try to understand me, Leela.
Leela	: From this day onwards, this door is closed for the Head Servitor. I have made

a mistake having faith in you. I have betrayed my God. I am *devadasi*... I am *devadasi*- I am only for God's enjoyment. Please forgive me, God...forgive me. I have made a mistake...I have made a mistake.

[Leelamayee sits down lamenting. Getting disturbed, Head Servitor leaves the place.]

SCENE-IX

[It's the dead of night. The Head Servitor is found lying on the road. While returning from *devadasi* Leelamayee's house, he consumed a lot and fell at a roadside. God meets him in his inebriated state.]

God : 'Head Servitor'…You?

Head Servitor : Who? Who's there?

God : (While coming from Iswar Nivas) Are you here in the dead of the night? Again, you're in this state?

Head Servitor : It's my wish that I can go anywhere. Who are you to obstruct me? I'm the Head Servitor at *Iswar Bhavan*. Among the servitors, I am the best. But you…Who are you?

God : I am God.

Head Servitor : But, why are you here in the dead of night? The main gate of Nivas is closed! How have you come out? Who has permitted you to come out?

God : If I ask you the same question?

Head Servitor : I am the great Servitor of *Ishwar Bhaban*. What I say is a rule for the *Bhavan*, and an unwritten constitution. I can ask others. But I can't be asked.

God : Be aware of your state, Head Servitor! Can you imagine if anybody sees you now at this state?

Head Servitor : Stop talking rubbish. I don't have time to listen to all this. Why are you here?

God : Do you browbeat me? You are grown up with my food sheltering under my arms. How ungrateful you are!

Head Servitor : I am the Head Servitor of *Ishwar Bhaban*. I don't take food free of cost. I do my duties. I wish I could do anything. Who are you to curb my rights? Every servitor of the *Ishwar Nivas* has a democratic right. Nobody can deprive him of that. I am here a respected citizen.

God : Tomorrow morning, when the city's people will know that the Head Servitor of *Ishwar Nivas* is an inebriated and henpecked man. How will you respond to them? Do you have any answer for that?

Head Servitor : The people will never get that opportunity. They can be hoodwinked or outwitted within five minutes. It's my warning to you.

God : Can you deny your illicit relationship with dancer Leelamayee?

Head Servitor	: I will never forgive you, if you interfere in my matters. It's my warning!
God	: Head Servitor, you are crossing your limits frequently. That day, you did not allow the couple hailing from Maharastra. Why had you deprived the Prime Minister of a country of this right!
Head Servitor	: They were of different religions.
God	: To me, all religions are equal. I am the God of coordinating all the religions.
Head Servitor	: These are all bookish knowledge and need to be updated. These are valueless and useless too.
God	: Head Servitor, there is an end to everything. You established your carnal relationship with my *devadasi*...you raped my devotee, Mary! How can you tell that this is justice?
Head Servitor	: If you are God, the omnipotent, why did you not obstruct me? Where was your divine power at that time? Where was your power hidden?
God	: I will wait until you reach the peak of your injustice. Enough is enough. You know it very well after that chapter.
Head Servitor	: Who is here to listen to your empty ideals? You know that you were Vishnu in the past. But in this modern age, that incarnation won't work. You are the most useless object and valueless soul for

today's man. Who asks you in this atomic age?

God : 'Head Servitor'!

Head Servitor : Ah!...stop shouting. God, you have done great injustice to *devadasi*, the royal dancer Leelamayee! Does she not have any life? Is she heartless? For how many days have you planned for an empty rendezvous with her body of flesh and blood? I have given her peace...I have given her happiness. I have made her holy.

God : My *devadasi* is holy and pure. I know her better than you. She has grown up with divine feelings and spirit. You have made her go astray. You have misled her.

Head Servitor : Don't tell lies, God. What have you given to her who has entirely dedicated her life to your service? Have you ever understood her heart? You are a lifeless stone! How can you know the agonies of human beings? You don't have any mind or any spirit? You are an immovable idol.

God : Head Servitor! Don't satirize me metaphorically. Can you imagine tomorrow morning, when the country's people will listen to your ignominy? Can you stand upright? How can you reply to their questions?

Head Servitor : I know the people of this country better than you. They believe more in the priests and the servitors than God. Their faith is the yardstick of my victory. Within no time, I can hypnotize them.

God : Head servitor! You forget your position and prestige. You have to stand in the people's court for the injustice you have shown toward Mary. You will be punished for that.

Head Servitor : Yes, you are talking of the people! Are you teaching me about those I direct for sit-ups? But, you remember, if I want, your *Ishwar Nivas* will be closed forever. Do you want to examine this?

God : Don't you repent that you have ruined the life of an innocent devotee? Don't you realize that you have committed a crime? Of what elements is your body composed? You are no longer a human. I severely condemn you, Head servitor!

Head Servitor : Who had permitted you to ask me this question? I am the controller of *Ishwar Nivas*. I am the Head Servitor, the representative of God. What I desire is an unwritten constitution of *Ishwar Nivas*. What I say is a rule for the dwellers of *Nivas*.

God : Only for your mischievousness, the holy place of God gets defamed and stigmatized. You have cheated the country's people after taking the liquor of religion. At last, you do your business in my name. How can you be so mean?

Head Servitor : Hold your tongue, God! There is no need to show your neat and clean image. I will publicly announce that your need at *Ishwar Nivas* has come to an end. We have to search for a new God. My words won't be only for the *Ishwar Nivas*. Its call will be spread from city to village, from slum to slum, to every forest dweller. You will see what answer will reach us.

God : Your pride won't last long Head Servitor! I will retake another incarnation, only for your destruction...for the release of the holy places of Gods and Goddesses from superstitions and unconditional beliefs.

Head Servitor : Before that, I will ruin *Ishwar Nivas*. Your idols will be entirely devastated on this earth. I will tell the people how you have changed yourself into a machine, God. Now you need a *nabakalebara* (replacement of old idols with the new ones). Prepare yourselves to celebrate the festival.

[Head Servitor starts laughing loudly. God gets agitated and firmly holds his ears like a typhoon passed nearby.]

SCENE-X

[It's the meeting hall of *Ishwar Nibas*. Among the present councillors are Venkatpati Raju, the Administrator and Head Priest. There is an important meeting on an urgent basis.]

Head Priest : Devotee best! If your dream is confirmed, a terrible result will come out soon. It will be disastrous.

V. Raju : Moreover, I am not the only one to see this dream. All of you have seen it. Then, we have to take serious action against the culprit.

Administrator : Yes, there is no question of telling a lie here. We are all unanimous at one point. The theme of everyone's dream is one.

V. Raju : Till now, the Head Servitor has not reached us. He has been away for long.

Administrator : Nobody can talk of him. We have to make an inquiry of the matter well before giving any final verdict. We must investigate and ascertain the root.

Head Priest : Having seen the God's face turning into

	black, my suspicion gets confirmed in the morning, *Rajashree*!
V. Raju	: It's the first issue in the history of *Ishwar Nivas*. It had never happened earlier.
Administrator	: Along with the Idol turning black, the perching of a vulture on the main entrance gate of *Ishwar Nivas*....having seen the cattle's head at the door...all these are signs of an ill omen here soon.
Head Priest	: The mishaps are marked one after another. How can we be silent?
V. Raju	: Mary's body is sent for post-mortem and doctor's examination. They will take serious action against the culprit if the allegations are confirmed. Can we restore our prestige in society? *Ishwar Nivas* will be treated as defamed and stigmatized as an unholy place. Why will the people and devotees respect me as the royal saint (*Rajashree*)? Yes, why will they respect me?
Head Priest	: That's not all. God's flute and *uttariya* (shawl) are also missing. The incident is mysterious. What do you think, Administrator?
Administrator	: In one day, so many incidents happen. But none of you is aware of them?
V. Raju	: The matter will undoubtedly worsen, if the incident is given any political coat. The political parties will gain momentum from this.

Head Priest	:	Then, what's the way?
V. Raju	:	I think of what to do next. I am disturbed now. I have never imagined such an incident to happen so quickly.
Administrator	:	On behalf of the *Ishwar Nivas*, we must give the general public our media bytes and statements about the mishap. But we should not differ in our opinions.
Head Priest	:	What opinion will you give, Administrator, Sir? The public is sure that an ignominy has happened at *Ishwar Nivas*. What will we say to make them understand? The blackening of God's Idol, the perching of a vulture at the main entrance point, seeing the cattle's head at the door- the message can reach everywhere very fast, and the people will think that these are happening because of infamies at *Ishwar Nivas*. These have never happened earlier. Why are these happening nowadays?
Administrator	:	Yes, nobody can hide the matter. It can't be suppressed at all.
V. Raju	:	Had you imposed the rules and regulations strictly for *Ishwar Nivas* earlier, such an incident wouldn't have happened! You are the representative of Government.
Administrator	:	I am just a rubber stamp. But, all activities are controlled by the servitors and priests. Head Priest won't disagree with the matter. Head Priest, please, you say. Is it a lie? Have I told you a lie?

Head Priest	: Yes, you are absolutely right.
V. Raju	: Then, why don't you revolt? Why are you silent? Why are you all silent, being the respected citizens of India? The people have enough support and conviction in you.
Administrator	: The general public of the country is afraid of religion. They are timid and the cowards. The race sheltering under the arms of God does not know how to revolt. That race knows only how to surrender.
V. Raju	: I am ashamed of this human race. It has been a common practice here to accept any incident unquestionably.
Head Priest	: The Head Servitor is approaching this side (looking in one direction).
Head Servitor	: I say Pranam to you, Rajashree!

[God's flute and *uttariya* are in the hands of the Head Servitor. They are all astonished to see.]

Head Priest	: Here is God's flute….Here is God's *uttariya* too. Then all these…
Administrator	: Where did you get all these?
Head Servitor	: That's a surprise.
V. Raju	: Head Servitor, where were you so long?
Head Servitor	: Where else can I be except the Police Station? The police picked up the dead body from the sea beach. They had also taken these two with them.
V. Raju	: This means all these-?

Head Servitor	: All these are taken along with the dead body of that woman.
Head Priest	: Are you sure, Head Servitor?
Head Servitor	: You couldn't recognize me after working so many days at *Ishwar Nivas*? Why are you so suspicious of my integrity?
V. Raju	: I can't believe this.
Head Servitor	: While the police took the dead body, I was there. I told them that these are our God's only. Of course, I was asked about this at the site of the incident. There was no other way except answering them rightly.
Administrator	: At least you could have informed us. All these happened…we couldn't know anything.
Head Servitor	: How could I get time? When I recognized these two, they immediately instructed me to sit in the vehicle and took me to the police station. I didn't get time to come to you.
V. Raju	: How come God's flute and *uttariya* reached there? Why were these there? All these seem to be mysterious.
Head Servitor	: The whole city is discussing the matter. I can't say what the people say. Leave it!
Head Priest	: The people's opinion-
Head Servitor	: Very…very bad! You can't listen to it. How will I speak? Please you move and enquire. You will hear them.

V. Raju	: What do the people discuss? Do they suspect God?
Head Servitor	: They do believe that this is God's work only. Long ago, God decreed in a dream to install an idol of Radha at the *Ishwar Nivas*. None of you did listen to Him.
V. Raju	: Yes, that's very old.
Head Servitor	: You should have brought the Idol of Radha. Now, you see the consequence.
V. Raju	: It's not the child's play to think of an idol of Radha weighing twenty kilograms of gold. Where will we get that huge amount? Why will I think about that after the maintenance responsibility is handed over to the Government? The trustees will decide.
Head Servitor	: Please, you say, *Rajashree*. How many days will God live alone without his female companion? His pangs of separation from Radha lead him to commit this heinous crime here.
Head Priest	: No…! That can't be. It is a fabricated story.
Administrator	: The creator of the Universe can't do this. It's just a conspiracy, well-plotted. God can never be so mean.
Head Priest	: This is just the propaganda campaigned to blame God and the conspiracy of a handful of people with their evil intentions. I have to reply to them firmly. Yes, we have to oppose them.

Head Servitor	: But why? Who will blame God for what? Has he harmed anybody?
Head Priest	: How has this incident reached the public? With what intension is one plotting this against the God? So strange incident!
Head Servitor	: That topic is discussed everywhere. Move anywhere; you will see the people are discussing God's character only. Nobody can hear this.
V. Raju	: Head Servitor, can you guess? Whose conspiracy can it be? Who is behind this? Suspicion gradually piles up. Who do you doubt?
Head Servitor	: You know it well that from the very beginning I am unmarried. I don't have any idea about the carnal desires. How can I tell you? It seems to me that a foreign hand is behind this.
Administrator	: This incident spreads from ear to ear. The whole world will know this.
Head servitor	: He could have easily escaped, if God's flute and *uttariya* that he wears had not been found. But now he is trapped. Because of these evidences, he is in danger.
V. Raju	: Someone else might have thrown them where Mary's dead body was found! What do you think, Head Priest? Maybe!
Head Priest	: That person must be of this *Ishwar Nivas* only. For whom God's character is now questioned.

Administrator : This is certainly different from an ordinary person's work and a well-plotted conspiracy.

V. Raju : Head Servitor, who do you doubt? Who can be behind this?

Head Servitor : Nobody can do this except God.

All three : No...this is a man's activity...the activity of a selfish and mean-minded person.

[All three have shouted simultaneously in one voice. The Head Servitor is unable to think what to do next. He starts running hurriedly. The light gets dimmed on stage.]

SCENE-XI

[Now, at the main entrance gate of *Ishwar Nivas* Joseph is sitting sadly. He is entirely morose and dejected. Some think that a beggar is waiting for people's sympathy. So, they drop coins towards him. It's the last quarter of the night. Joseph is waiting for Mary. After the stage light, Mary's dead body is in God's hand. God is standing before Joseph. There is a slight dim light on stage.]

God : Joseph…Joseph…get up, my son. Get up, my devotee.

[Joseph is shocked.]

Joseph : Who? Mary, why are you so late? My eyes are full of tears and waiting for you. Nobody answers me, when I ask them about you. Who are you, Sir? Where was my Mary so long?

God : (Silent and flood of tears continuously shedding down) Joseph…

Joseph : Why are you crying, my son? You have brought back my Mary…that's enough. I don't need anything more.

[God puts Mary's dead body in Joseph's lap. Joseph can't accept this as a dead body. But he thinks that Mary is sleeping in his lap as usual.]

Joseph	: Mary…Mary…Mary…Get up…after one hour, the darkness will disappear. We will return to our native place. Mami (Aunt) must be waiting for us. She will be thrilled to have seen us after a long time! Hey, you get up, Mary. The night is over. We have to reach the railway platform.
God	: Mary won't get up at all, Joseph. She has slept permanently. She will never say anything.
Joseph	: Why, Sir? What has happened to my Mary? Why won't she open her mouth?
God	: I couldn't help you, Joseph. I have been defeated. Yes, ultimately, I have been defeated. Please, forgive me.
Joseph	: Who are you, Sir? Please let me know you first. You have returned to me my Mary, but you are yet to reveal your identity.
God	: I am God. For whom you have come here covering a long distance. But I couldn't do anything for my devotee. I repent that.
Joseph	: [Silently, he looks at Mary for a while. He can't think of what to do next.]
God	: I am the culprit, Joseph. My identity is redundant and valueless when I can't save my devotee. The crime committed today is only because of me. It won't be repeated in future.

Joseph	:	But why, Lord?
God	:	I know, Joseph, you have been hurt. Can anyone be healthy and in good condition after such an incident? But I promise you that I will take an incarnation in future for the destruction of evil ones on this earth.
Joseph	:	But-?
God	:	Don't question, Joseph. Today, I have been defeated. I can't return to *Ishwar Nivas* again with this bodily form. You will never come to this marble statue installed at *Nishwar Nivas*...that's made unholy. Yes...yes...unholy.

[Head Servitor reaches there swiftly. He looks at me sarcastically. God breaks down as if he were a culprit before the Head Servitor. God gets disturbed.]

Head Servitor	:	Wow...! You have essayed an excellent play. Remember that *Ishwar Nivas* is permanently closed for you, as you have touched the dead body of the person of a different religion. You have been sinful, God. Your divine spirit is lost.
God	:	Head Servitor, I will take another incarnation (as of Vishnu) for the destruction of people like you and your pride. I will come to neutralize the evil and nurture the good. With the collapse of vice, the virtue will reign glaringly.
Head Servitor	:	But *Ishwar Nivas* is prohibited for you. You may be worshipped somewhere else.

	Remember this. Nobody will ask you, if you are worshipped elsewhere.
God	: I strongly condemn the places where the mischievous priests, servitors, Mullahs, and knowledgeable persons are seen. You are all the culprits.
Head Servitor	: *Ishwar Nivas* will be worshipped without God since this day. Till the time statue remains, there is no need of you, God. Your figure is more important and valuable than you for our stomach.
God	: But, my *nabakalebar* (new form replacing the old one) is inevitable. The signs of the age (of change) can't be checked and blocked by you, Head Servitor! You can't stop the deluge that rises beneath the horizon.
Head Servitor	: That day may never come, God, for you are imprisoned in the hands of people.

[Like a dumb person, Joseph listens to their arguments but unable to understand. Head Servitor and God accuse each other.]

| God | : Remember, Head Servitor! After I leave, *Ishwar Nivas* will be the resting place of vultures and owls. How many days will you baffle and hoodwink the people, selling my images in the name of religion? Head Servitor! The day the ordinary people will know that the idols installed at the Temple, Mosque, Church and Gurdwar are meant only for the stomachs |

of servitors, priests, and learned men, their malice will end that day. They will never forgive you all that day.

Head Servitor : Perhaps that day won't come. Till the day the mantras of the Gita, the Bible, and the Koran are in our hearts, the people will obey us. We are servitors…priests… protectors of society…living idols of God…the incarnation of God. Hah…hah…hah…

[He laughs loudly.]

[Joseph clasps Mary tightly. God disappears from that spot. Darkness comes in.]

SCENE-XII

[Any place of the city is, of course, crowded, considered here. Joseph is sitting unhappily. Suleiman, a leader of the Muslim religion, tries to make him understand. Joseph remains unchanged. But Suleiman tries his best to influence him unendingly.]

Suleiman : It's not the time for you to mourn over the death of Mary and break down, Joseph! You have to wake up and take revenge for our God...for our religion...for our community...for our race...!

Joseph : What will we earn, Suleiman? My Mary won't come back again. For whom will I take revenge? Why will I take revenge?

Suleiman : One Mary has gone. But, now thousands of Maries still wait for you in the country. Do you want them to suffer the foul-smelling agonies of hell? Do you want them to be victimized in the name of religion? Do you want them to sacrifice their lives?

Joseph : Suleiman, the animal can't walk straight once the spine gets broken. Mary's murder

	has drained all my energy and made me powerless. I am utterly helpless.
Suleiman	: No, Joseph…No…! You have to raise your voice against this injustice for Mary only …for the right of Christianity…to respect man like a man. As a free citizen, you must live with honour and prestige.
Joseph	: Suleiman…!
Suleiman	: Yes, Joseph, please have faith in you. Build up your self-confidence.
Joseph	: I strongly denied her, but she didn't listen to me. She came to see God…

[While saying, Joseph cries.]

Suleiman	: Joseph, forget the past. Be ready for the present. When the country wants battle from us, we can't sit silently. The race seeks explanation from us…seeks justice…
Joseph	: Is there any taste of the curry that is already burnt? Why will I interfere in all those matters? Mary won't return…
Suleiman	: Why do you think of this as a personal issue? Today, they have done injustice towards Christianity. Tomorrow, they will do the same for the Muslim religion. After that, they will disobey the Sikh religion. How many days will you live flogged? It's better to fight than to bear. While fighting, embracing death is not a loss.

Joseph	: Can you live peacefully fighting against the majority Hindu community? Who will help us? For this, the power…money …needed, all that…?
Suleiman	: Why will we neglect our duties, when victory and defeat are subservient to Time? We will fight, until we shed the last drop of blood. First of all, we will stand united. Then, automatically, the road will be clear to us.
Joseph	: There is a sea gap between what we speak and do. A herculean task…Can it be possible?
Suleiman	: Dreaming of defeat in life, nobody can rise. So, listen to your heart and let your soul be exposed to the exploration of light, at least once. Do the people of minority communities have no individuality? Can't you do this much for them?
Joseph	: Minority! Ah…! Suleiman, why is my body with a causeless vibration? All the veins of my body are torn apart. What can be the cause of this vibration? What can be?
Suleiman	: That vibration wants the right and the authority. That needs freedom. Let that be directed upward, Joseph. 'Right' doesn't depend upon anybody's sympathy. That is to be snatched away. Yes…yes… forcibly.
Joseph	: Yes…yes…I can, Suleiman. I can certainly

	do that. I am not weak at all. I will fight… indeed I will fight.
Suleiman	: Bravo…friend…bravo! I know if you are conscious within, nobody can obstruct it. The people can be aware of this consciousness everywhere. It is our duty.
Joseph	: But, where's the way?
Suleiman	: In the name of religion…within the community, everything is possible in the country. The upcoming election is very close. We have to prepare ourselves for that day. This incident will be the best manifesto of that election.
Joseph	: What do you mean?
Suleiman	: This time, we won't consider selecting a candidate unanimously. This Municipality Election will subsequently influence the State Assembly and Parliamentary Elections.
Joseph	: This time, the vote is sure to divide.
Suleiman	: Head Servitor is a candidate in the election this time. He has taken this for granted; all the votes will be in his favour in the name of religion. Before that, well in advance, we will plan accordingly-
Joseph	: We will be united first among the minority communities. It is our big responsibility.
Suleiman	: For that, I want to use you as a weapon. Having heard your mournful story, the voters of the minority communities will

                    store their shingles and pebbles and pelt against them instead of voting.

Joseph   : What an idea! Thanks, Suleiman... Thanks!

[Both of them shake their hands very happily. Then, the prayers from the Mosque and Church are heard at a distance. In the meantime, the stage is lit off.]

SCENE-XIII

[A crowded place of the city is used as the courtyard for the elections. The candidates show their different strategies for the final day of the election. Both the candidates, the Head Servitor and Suleiman, request and invite the voters to vote in their favour. From the background, they heard a big round of applause and support for their favourite candidates. On both sides of the front part of the stage are standing two candidates in the style of declaring their manifestoes publicly.]

Head Servitor : Brothers, my victory is the people's victory. My victory is the victory of God Himself. You know very well what I have not done for this city! What I have not done for *Ishwar Nivas*! What I have not done for you!

[From the background is heard a big round of applause.]

Suleiman : Brothers, I don't request you to vote me. I invite you for justice. Please, you say, for how many days the corruption will continue in the name of religion? That day, having ruined Mary's life, her dead body was thrown on the sea beach.

But what matters here most is that God was blamed for this ignominy. Can a vile incident of this kind happen at the *Ishwar Nivas*, which stands on the path of righteousness, truth and justice? God is ours. He is not of the Hindus...not of the Muslims...not of the Christians only. He is of the human race...of the whole world.

[He is supported with a big round of applause.]

Head Servitor : Brothers, I am unmarried throughout my life. Have you not recognized the person who has been serving you all... who has been serving the afflicted people of the society? The servitor of the people... servitor of God...this is the Head Servitor. You have all given me the right to serve you. If you think this Head Servitor of God is the most ineligible candidate in the courtyard of the election, I am ready to withdraw my nomination today.

[There is a huge round of applause and the approval of phrases like "Head servitor...Zindabad".]

Suleiman : Brothers, I help you remember the anecdote of the innocent woman Mary. What did she get having come to see God here? She is not a Christian; she is the sister of the entire human race...mother... wife...! Had it happened that day in the Hindu religion, would you have forgiven the culprit, the murderer? Please do think about it. Who was the main hero of this incident? Who did raise this incident first? Would you welcome the person who ruined the chastity of girls and daughters-in-law of your society in the darkness of night and reads the Gita, the Bhagabat, the Bible and the Koran in the broad day light? Please say...please answer my questions...

[From the background is heard- "Our candidate Suleiman-Zindabad".]

Head Servitor : Brothers, my opponent has expressed comments about my character. You know well what my character is. If the Head Servitor who has observed celibacy throughout his life is blamed for his character for the last incident committed a few days ago, you don't vote for me. It's my humble request to you all that, not being tempted by any means, please cast vote for me. Let me serve you all at least once.

Suleiman : Brothers, it's the time now. You all decide, please. Stay aware of the splendour and brilliant speech and lecture. Select the servitor who will be your friend in your need, but not the Head Servitor whose place is already fixed at the *Ishwar Nivas*. The servitor to the distressed people can't be the Head Servitor! Battlefield is ready. You are all the suitable jury members.

[Along with the round of applause a stone is pelted and hurt the forehead of Suleiman. It is bleeding. There is a clamour and chaos among the audience. Still, Suleiman delivers his speech.]

Joseph : (Getting up the stage) It's not the time to get oppressed, brothers...You all decide, please. Some selfish people of the Hindu religion have threatened to kill Suleiman. Today, you see in your eyes the condition of Suleiman. Disguising in the name of religion, one can't be the public representative. Please end the fight and resolve the conflict beforehand. Please support and vote for justice.

[Head Servitor comes to Joseph on the stage. Because of the tussle, the Head Servitor falls. The Administrator comes to the stage, and suddenly, he shoves Suleiman. In this fight, on one side are Suleiman and Joseph; while on the other side are Head Servitor and Administrator. God reaches there in the middle of the battle. Then, the acting becomes symbolic.]

God : No...! It's not good to quarrel between brothers. I don't want you to fight for me in my name. You all calm down and be seated.

[The people of both communities observe God for a while. They ask questions frequently without recognizing him.]

Suleiman : 'You'?

God : Have you forgotten me? I am God...your God.

Suleiman : Why have you come? Have you come to enjoy our enmity and bitterness?

Head Servitor	: Having reached here, you have made a mistake. Go...go away. Who has permitted you to come here?
Suleiman	: For you, only this bloodshed is here today. Yes, well. You take the decision today, who will live here? Whether the Hindus or the Muslims?
God	: You are all making mistakes! Why is this bloodshed...the unnecessary fight in my name for me? Try to understand me.
Suleiman	: You are the opportunist. You are selfish.
Head Servitor	: You have to tell the public today. You say whether you are for the Hindus, the Muslims, the Christians, or the Sikhs.
God	: I am for all the people, the whole world... for the entire human race. Why are they fighting here for me? Please-
Head servitor	: No, that can't be. For ages, God was for the Hindus, is for the Hindus and will be for Hindus. For you, I have created innumerable fairs, festivals, and mahotsavs. Are these practices useless or valueless? Answer me, God. Why are you silent?
Suleiman	: For you, I am celebrating Id, Ramjan. Are these of no value?
God	: But I don't want them all. You have made all these arrangements for your interests.
Head Servitor	: Nothing was arranged for your interest. That day it wasn't; today, it isn't.

God	: What do you want to say?
Suleiman	: You are immovable and static. I have instilled life in you. Can you deny this, God?
Head Servitor	: I have generated an indomitable spirit and aspirations to live in you. Let me know if I need to correct something.
Suleiman	: The works I have done so far are only for you. For your interest, I have disguised and masked myself. I have acted.
God	: What do you say? Try to understand me at least once.
Head Servitor	: Try to remember how you had been recognized publicly in the world. Why are you hesitant to accept this?
Suleiman	: I have written the holy Koran to please you. I have done a lot to make the Koran recognized in the world.
God	: You all have misunderstood me! Try to recognize me at least once. See my heart. Look at my inner feelings.
Head Servitor	: Why do you hesitate to express the truth? Had I been a miser for you that day? Speak frankly without any fear. You are entirely for the Hindus. You are for the Hindu race and the Hindu religion.
Suleiman	: No, that can't be. You are for the Muslim religion. I have given up everything for you. But, now, you can't betray me. You

are for the Muslims...For you, I have created Iraq, Iran, Arab, and Pakistan... You are for the Muslims.

Head Servitor : 'For the Hindus'...

Suleiman : 'For the Muslims'...

[God has advised them to be calm and quiet. But, none of them obeys this.]

Head Servitor : 'For the Hindus'...

Suleiman : 'For Muslims'...

[From the background, an announcement is read out.]

Announcement: The Government has announced that the country's people should be vigilant for the celebration of laying the foundation stone of Ram-Mandir organized today. The State Government of Bihar has taken stringent actions against the agitations raised in twelve districts, while the stone for Ram is brought and worshipped. All the schools and colleges of the state are closed. The police report says that three dead bodies were rescued from Rotas Police Station. Fifteen persons were arrested on the accusation of riot and violence. The non-official report says the number of bodies killed in riots is only eight.

[After the announcement, the people of two communities' gheraoed God, flagellated him and started fighting among themselves. God falls down, having heard the firing of bullets ceaselessly. Others left the spot injured. The stage is gradually dimmed with light. In that darkness are heard the clamour, the sound of bombing and women's cry of distress.]

SCENE-XIV

[The stage is flooded with lights. Then, on the stage are all other characters except God and Master. They are in different postures of their bodies while acting.]

[The blue light will revolve around the stage. The characters that will be spotted with this blue light can be active, whereas at other places, other characters will be marked with red light and in normal conditions.]

['Blue' light is to be followed one by the announcement. Acting will also be continued, when the information is read out from the background. Focusing on the report, based on the feelings, acting will be displayed. Announcements will be publicized successively.]

First Announcement

"As per the news report, because of violence and riots all over the country of Babri-Masjid destruction, at least three hundred people have died. But the death toll goes beyond this, according to the non-official report. Most people died in the metropolitan city of Bombay out of violence, stabbing and police firing. Approximately two hundred people are under treatment in the hospital, and most are very critical. The death toll may increase."

[The Samaj dated 09.12.1992]

Action

[In the 'blue' light zone will be the Administrator and Joseph doing the role of police. One person will lathi-charge and the other will fire the pistol. Suleiman will stab Venkatpati Raju. The Head Servitor and Head Priest will fight among themselves. Leelamayee and Mary must cry, keeping their heads down. One has lost her husband, and the other will be at some loss. Following the announcement, all these actions will be continued. When the report reading is stopped, the characters will be neutral.]

Second Announcement

[When the second light zone is focused, the acting under 'blue' light will be closed and put under the red zone. That means when it is expected, the theatre will again start in the second 'blue' light zone along with the announcement.]

"One government spokesperson says that the Idol of Lord Ram is safe and intact in the half-built temple by the devotees (*Karasevaks*)...it can be mentioned that the Ram Temple is already under construction after removing the debris of Babri masjid yesterday. The Idol of Ramlala is founded in the temple. The secretary of Ramjanmabhumi Muktijajna Samiti, Sri Mahesh Narayan, says that a traditional canopy (Chandua) is to be hung over the Idol after its proper installation. Riot-controlling Rapid Action Force, first breaking through the obstacles, reaches the controversial spots. After rescuing the devotees (Karasevaks) immediately, they control the mass agitation."

[The Samaj dated 09.12.1992]

Action

[In the 'blue' light zone, some people are shown destroying the Mosque. Subsequently, some people will bring Ramlala to the throne with the sound of gongs and drumbeats. Bending down the neck, waist and knee, Ramalala will sit on the throne while smiling gently. Then, the chanting of hymns in praise of the Lord is continued by the devotees. After a while, the Police Force will enter the spot and lathi-charge the devotees gathered there. But Ramalala will sit as usual. All these actions will be executed as per the second announcement.]

Third Announcement

"Today, because of strong protest for twenty-five minutes in Loksabha, the normal activities are postponed for a week on the third day of the Parliamentary Session. ...Prime Minister Sri P. V. Narasingh Rao announced yesterday that an Enquiry Committee to be constituted soon to investigate the matters about the dismantling of Babri-masjid and other matters of this sort and to take appropriate action against the suspended Chief Minister of Uttar Pradesh, Sri Kalyan Singh...The President of SAARC and the President of Srilanka Sri Ransingh Premadas, has announced that because of the incidents happening in Ayodhya and the subsequent situations all over India, and the Prime Minister of India, Sri Narasigh Rao's inability to attend this meeting, the conference has been postponed."

[The Samaj dated 10.12.1992]

Action

[There will be strong arguments continued among the members of Loksabha. The President, Hon'ble Speaker Loksabha, tries his best to control the situation. The Prime Minister's announcement for the constitution of the Enquiry Committee, Bajpayee's warning, Premadas's announcement, etc, will be displayed through acting. Action will be continued in the 'blue' light zone.]

LAST SCENE

[A slight dim light is on the stage. All the characters are found dead. Some are stabbing others, while others are firing. Some of them are lathi-charging. Some of them are fighting among themselves. Some are with tearful eyes, while some are fainted. Regaining consciousness time and again, they lose their sense again. All other characters show the events except God and Master.]

[God comes down slowly to that spot. He's with a bandage on his forehead. It bleeds. He has come to observe each event with utmost care and cries. After enquiring all the circumstances, he comes to the front of the stage. He sits while crying.]

[Master comes beating the drum to the stage. Dimmed light disappears. Then there's normal light on stage. All the characters surround God. This time, Master starts his traditional announcement.]

Master : O, Ladies and Gentlemen! You think that my work still continues! You have seen the onset of the play, but people are yet to determine its end. Meanwhile, I am searching for God for ages. I am unaware of his whereabouts. He is missing. I have circulated the message through radio, television and newspapers. But nobody has replied me about him. If you come across him anywhere, you will report me immediately.

Yes, for your kind information, he won't come so quickly. He is a scoundrel. If I find him anywhere, I will drag him, putting a towel upon his neck. One more request is that you never report him to the police station. I will thrash him the way I want. You won't speak to him anything. I will tell him what I have to…This time I will screw him. Where will he go?

[Master beats the drum loudly. The stage is lit off.]

END

Black Eagle Books

www.blackeaglebooks.org
info@blackeaglebooks.org

Black Eagle Books, an independent publisher, was founded as a nonprofit organization in April, 2019. It is our mission to connect and engage the Indian diaspora and the world at large with the best of works of world literature published on a collaborative platform, with special emphasis on foregrounding Contemporary Classics and New Writing.

www.ingramcontent.com/pod-product-compliance
Lightning Source LLC
Chambersburg PA
CBHW060618080526
44585CB00013B/885